The Expert's Guide to

Buying a House in the UK:

helping you to buy a good home and a good property investment.

by

Dr Judith Summer
of
Simma Properties

Simma Properties - Finding your little property treasure
Copyright © 2016 Judith Penina Summer
All rights reserved.

The Expert's Guide to Buying a House in the UK:
helping you to buy a good home and a good property investment.
by Dr Judith Summer.

Copyright and Disclaimer

All rights reserved. No part of this publication may be reproduced, stored in a retrieval system, or transmitted, in any form or by any means electronic, mechanical, photocopying, recording or otherwise, without the prior written permission of Judith Penina Summer.

I can be contacted via my website at http://www.simmaproperties.co.uk

Whilst every effort has been made to ensure that the information contained in this book is correct, the author cannot accept any responsibility for any errors or omissions or for any consequences resulting therefrom.

Whilst I hope to be able to help you, I cannot be held responsible or liable in contract or in tort or in any way if there are any inaccuracies in this book and/or if my advice does not work for you and/or your circumstances. All I can say is that my approach works for me and has helped me to build a successful property portfolio. I hope it may guide you in similar successes, although of course there is no guarantee. This book does not contain tailored advice for your particular circumstances and I do not pretend to know what the market conditions in your area are like either now or in the future. Please do not construe any advice given in this book as a command or a rule or a statement of fact. My advice is mere guidance to be adapted by you as necessary in all the circumstances of the case, and it reflects my opinions. The opinions I express are my own, and you may well disagree with them. Remember that buying and selling property is more of an art than a science, and there are no formulae or hard and fast rules as to what works best in any particular circumstance. You must not rely on information in this book as an alternative to legal or other qualified professional advice. This disclaimer will be governed by and construed in accordance with English law, and any disputes relating to this disclaimer will be subject to the exclusive jurisdiction of the courts of England and Wales.

Simma Properties - Finding your little property treasure
Copyright © 2016 Judith Penina Summer
All rights reserved.

**The Expert's Guide to Buying a House in the UK:
helping you to buy a good home and a good property investment.
by Dr Judith Summer.**

Blurb

In 12 easy digestible chapters, this book covers what to look for in buying your next home, whether it is a flat or a house. A good home should also make a good property investment. This book should empower you to value the property you want, yourself, without relying on estate agents, and to understand how the system works in England and Wales. It explains about how to work out what you can afford, getting a mortgage and options for first time buyers. This book gives advice on bidding, negotiating, gazumping, hidden costs and conveyancing in England and Wales, and also sets out property development issues to consider. Each chapter concludes with a summary of top tips.

There is a sister book written by me: The Expert's Guide to Selling a House in the UK: helping you to sell well. This can also be found on Amazon Kindle. I have made an effort not to duplicate the information in each book.

Further books may follow!

In the meantime, my blog and property finding services can be accessed via my website: http://www.simmaproperties.co.uk/index.php and you can find my TV interviews for Sky's Property Panorama on my YouTube Channel (Judith Summer at Simma Properties).

Enjoy!

Simma Properties - Finding your little property treasure
Copyright © 2016 Judith Penina Summer
All rights reserved.

The Expert's Guide to Buying a House in the UK:
helping you to buy a good home and a good property investment.
by Dr Judith Summer.

Contents

Copyright and Disclaimer
Blurb
Contents
Introduction
  Overview
  How do I know what I am talking about?
  This book and its sister book
Chapter 1
How do you buy the right property for you?
  1.1   Write a list
  1.2   Location
  1.3   School catchment areas
  1.4   Parking
  1.5   Outside space
  1.6   Kitchen/living space
  1.7   Needs renovation
  1.8   New builds
  1.9   Investment value
  1.10 Summary top tips
Chapter 2
How do you find properties?
  2.1   Online search
  2.2   Register with agents
  2.3   How estate agents work
  2.4   Be proactive
  2.5   Viewings
  2.6   Buying agents
  2.7   Auctions
  2.8   Summary top tips
Chapter 3
How do you work out the value of the property?
  3.1   Three choices
  3.2   Research sold prices
  3.3   Price per square foot

The Expert's Guide to Buying a House in the UK:
helping you to buy a good home and a good property investment.
by Dr Judith Summer.

    3.4   Summary top tips

Chapter 4

Affordability and buying costs

    4.1   Youth, prospects and payment protection insurance
    4.2   Spending versus earnings: how much is left over?
    4.3   Level of mortgage
    4.4   Deposit
    4.5   Extra buying costs
        4.5.1   Stamp duty in the UK.
        4.5.2   Your solicitors' fees and expenses
        4.5.3   Buildings insurance (for a house)
        4.5.4   Mortgage fees
        4.5.5   House building surveys
        4.5.6   Removal costs
        4.5.7   Any repairs/ refurbishment
        4.5.8   Post redirection
        4.5.9   The costs of running a home
    4.6   Summary top tips

Chapter 5

Mortgages

    5.1   Mortgage in principle
    5.2   Process and terms
    5.3   Independent mortgage brokers
    5.4   Mortgage fees
    5.5   Speed
    5.6   Buy to let mortgages
    5.7   Government help schemes
        5.7.1   Help to Buy
        5.7.2   Starter Homes
        5.7.3   Shared Ownership
        5.7.4   First Time Buyer's Initiative
        5.7.5   Help to Buy ISA
        5.7.6   Lifetime ISA
        5.7.7   Right to Buy Scheme
    5.8   The Bank of Mum and Dad
    5.9   Summary top tips

Simma Properties - Finding your little property treasure

Copyright © 2016 Judith Penina Summer

All rights reserved.

**The Expert's Guide to Buying a House in the UK:
helping you to buy a good home and a good property investment.
by Dr Judith Summer.**

Chapter 6
What to find out from the agent
- 6.1 Why are they selling?
- 6.2. Are they motivated to sell?
- 6.3. Are there any bids on the property.
- 6.4 The agent cannot lie?
- 6.5 Summary top tips

Chapter 7
Top tips when viewing a property
- 7.1 Your wish list
- 7.2. See a property you like more than once
- 7.3 Turn the lights off in the day.
- 7.4 Phone reception
- 7.5 TV reception
- 7.6 Water pressure
- 7.7 Don't get distracted by the condition of the property, good or bad
- 7.8. Judge the house on its more permanent characteristics
- 7.9 Major turn-offs
- 7.10. Does the survey support your choice?
- 7.11 Summary top tips

Chapter 8
Other investigations
- 8.1 The neighbours
- 8.2. Noise
- 8.3 Local crime
- 8.4 Maintenance
- 8.5 Website searches
- 8.6 Summary top tips

Chapter 9
Bidding for a property
- 9.1 Factors to consider
- 9.2 See how the agent responds
- 9.3 Offers in writing
- 9.4 How high should you go?
- 9.5 Final bids
- 9.6 Mortgage valuation

Simma Properties - Finding your little property treasure
Copyright © 2016 Judith Penina Summer
All rights reserved.

**The Expert's Guide to Buying a House in the UK:
helping you to buy a good home and a good property investment.
by Dr Judith Summer.**

    9.7   Should you be the first bidder?
    9.8   Gazumping and moratoriums on marketing/ lock out agreements
    9.9   Sealed bids and competitive bids
    9.10   Summary top tips

Chapter 10
How to buy a house if you are in a chain
    10.1   What is a chain?
    10.2   Advantages of being chain free
    10.3   Disadvantages of making yourself chain free
    10.4   How to try to keep your end of the chain in motion
    10.5   Bridging finance
    10.6   Summary top tips

Chapter 11
Development
    11.1   Buying with a development in mind
    11.2   Permissions
    11.3   Enhancing the value
    11.4   Neutral decor
    11.5   Development for own use or for re-sale
    11.6   Summary top tips

Chapter 12
The conveyancing process
    12.1   How long do you need to find a property?
    12.2   Exchange and completion in England and Wales
    12.3   Things that slow down exchange
    12.4   Two week exchanges
    12.5   Contract race
    12.6   Summary top tips
Epilogue

Simma Properties - Finding your little property treasure
Copyright © 2016 Judith Penina Summer
All rights reserved.

The Expert's Guide to Buying a House in the UK:
helping you to buy a good home and a good property investment.
by Dr Judith Summer.

Introduction

Overview

How do I know what I am talking about?

This book and its sister book

Overview

The UK is experiencing high property prices and fierce competition in the residential market as demand for housing continues to far outweigh supply. The results of the referendum for the UK to leave the EU do not change this. In this book I aim to help buyers find their dream home for the right price. Markets can do strange things, so there are absolutely no promises about future investment values. All I can say is that if you buy right, that should mitigate, at least to some extent, against market downturns.

This book should help buyers from all walks of life, whether they are first time buyers or buyers who have bought before, and whether they would like to buy a small flat or a large house in the UK. It is based on the accumulation of my experience in a strong and vibrant market. I will give general advice such as what to look for in a property, as well as an overview of the legal system for conveyancing particular to England and Wales.

How do I know what I am talking about?

Trust me, I'm a lawyer! Actually I am a non-practising solicitor with a Cambridge degree in law and a PhD in law.

**The Expert's Guide to Buying a House in the UK:
helping you to buy a good home and a good property investment.
by Dr Judith Summer.**

But I also have nearly a decade of experience in investing in the property market of a prime residential area of central London. I have learnt to spot and buy a bargain for my own portfolio and I know how to sell a property so as to achieve a record price per square foot on the particular road.

I founded Simma Properties and now also act as a property finder and development consultant, spreading my expertise as far as I can. It may interest you to follow my twitter account @simmaproperties where I tweet about current UK property market news and trends. I have also appeared on Sky television giving property advice. I write a property blog via Tumblr which can be found at:
http://www.tumblr.com/blog/judithsummer
or
http://www.simmaproperties.co.uk/blog.php

This book and its sister book

This book is about buying a home in the UK. I have tried to include everything that I think is relevant, although of course there may be some things that I have not thought to add.

As mentioned above, there is also a separate sister book about selling a home in the UK. But it will help a seller to know what a buyer should be doing, and it will help a buyer to know what a seller should be doing, so feel free to buy both books! I have aimed to make it so that information contained in one book is not repeated in the other.

The Expert's Guide to Buying a House in the UK:
helping you to buy a good home and a good property investment.
by Dr Judith Summer.

Chapter 1

How do you buy the right property for you?

1.1   Write a list

1.2   Location

1.3   School catchment areas

1.4   Parking

1.5   Outside space

1.6   Kitchen/living space

1.7   Needs renovation

1.8   New builds

1.9   Investment values

1.10 Summary top tips

The right property has to be the one that is right for YOU. If it is going to be your home first and foremost, you should be thinking about where you want to live and what sort of amenities you would like your home to have.

So you have to decide what is important to you.

The Expert's Guide to Buying a House in the UK:
helping you to buy a good home and a good property investment.
by Dr Judith Summer.

1.1   Write a list

It sounds ridiculous, but it is a really good idea to make a written list. Then only look at properties in your price bracket that fulfil your criteria or most of your criteria. You should write the list in order of what is most important to you. If you have to make concessions in the end, either due to availability or affordability, so be it, but at least you will know what you are aiming for instead of being faced with hundreds of potential properties, estate agents pushing you to waste your time viewing everything and nothing really feeling right.

Everyone's list will be different, but here follow some factors to think about.

1.2   Location

This will usually be the single most important factor. Think about what things you want to live near. Think about the commute to work. It will make a big difference to your life if your walk to the station every day, twice a day, is 15 minutes longer than it used to be. Perhaps mark on a map the area in which you would consider living and at least at the beginning of your quest limit the search to this area. This might be something like anything within a half mile of a station. If you cannot find anything, or anything you can afford, and you are not prepared to wait, you can always enlarge your search area.

Of course, the search will be much easier if you know the general area in which you would like to live. However, if you do not know, http://www.findahood.com may be a useful tool so you can search for a suitable area based on what is important to you, such as good schools or low crime rates. http://www.commutefrom.com/ allows you to search for areas within a certain commute time from the central London station nearest to your work, based on how long you are prepared the commute to take and your budget for a new home. http://locationcounts.co.uk/ is another online tool to help you make up your mind about where in the UK you might want to live. You set out where roughly in the country you would like to live, set up your preferences and the website will display a "heat map" showing which areas are likely to meet your needs.

**The Expert's Guide to Buying a House in the UK:
helping you to buy a good home and a good property investment.
by Dr Judith Summer.**

If you want to ask local people questions about an area to move to outside of London, you can pose questions on the forum at http://www.lifeafterlondon.com/ .

1.3 School catchment areas

Do you want to live in an urban area? If you have a pre-school child, or you might have one in the near future, and you want him/her to go to a state school or voluntary aided religious school, or for an older child, a grammar school or a particular state school, you have to be in the right catchment area to have even the slightest chance of getting in. Some online property listing sites also indicate proximity to the local schools eg under the "local info" tab of a property listed on Zoopla. If in doubt, telephone the school of your choice and ask about entrance criteria and catchment areas.

Yes, you need to research schools if you are moving house even if the possibility of pregnancy is just a far distant and scary prospect on the horizon. For the record, having a child is a much scarier prospect if you have not already done some research about this!

You can also look at individual school performances and tables via the Department of Education's tool at https://www.compare-school-performance.service.gov.uk/ and read the Ofsted reports of the school you are interested in at http://reports.ofsted.gov.uk/

1.4 Parking

If you have a car, or think you might have one soon, you will want to be able to park it at or near your new place. In some areas, this is not a problem as there will be multiple, unfettered, free spaces in the road outside at all times. However, if you want to live in a city, especially towards the centre, parking gets a lot trickier. You do not want to be driving round and round after a night out, trying to spot a space to park. You do not want to be lugging your shopping to your door after a 5 mile hike from your parking space.

**The Expert's Guide to Buying a House in the UK:
helping you to buy a good home and a good property investment.
by Dr Judith Summer.**

You will have to decide what sort of parking facility you need: a covered garage for your special car; a driveway for ease or access; street parking; or residents' only street parking. If you are not sure if there is enough residents' street parking, drive around the area and see how easy it would be to park at different times of the day and night.

When you buy a property, do not assume that you will automatically get residents' parking rights: some properties do not come with any, especially some newer builds or new conversions in densely populated urban areas like Camden or Brent in London.

Even if the property or the street does not have parking, it might be worth seeing if there are any parking facilities that you can buy or rent nearby, although as this may not be a permanent arrangement, it may not work for you. There are specialist websites to search on such as http://en.parkopedia.co.uk/ or http://www.parklet.co.uk/.

If you do not need a parking space, then this is only a question which could affect the re-saleability of your purchase. If there is no parking, the property should be priced accordingly cheaper, and you will need to balance affordability and the need for parking.

1.5 Outside space

Having some outside space is a must for me, having lived in a flat without a balcony or communal garden, which was also not near a park. This drove me mad, especially as I worked in an office all week and I like walking outside even if it is cold. If being outside does not bother you, then it will not matter so much for you. Most flats do not have outside space. It also might be something you have to compromise on. If you have children and you can afford some outside space, it would be better, especially if you do not have a nearby park.

1.6 Kitchen/living space

The hub of most homes, especially one with children, is the kitchen/living area. Look at the space available or the potential space of this area and think about whether it will

be enough for you. If you cook every meal, you need a bigger kitchen than if you more commonly microwave ready meals. Are you often catering for ten, or is it usually just two of you?

1.7 Needs renovation

People often have unrealistic expectations of themselves and what work they would be prepared to undertake on a property. Properties which need renovation are going to be cheaper than ones which don't, although the overall cost of buying it and doing it up might be the same as buying it already done. Just be careful when you are doing your estimates.

Sometimes a property which has been renovated, especially a new build, is overpriced - maybe up to 20%, so do your research on property values (see below). You do not necessarily want to be paying a premium for someone else's taste in paint.

Some people say they would happily refurbish a property but are attracted in reality only to the ones which have already been refurbished. Others say they do not want to have to do any work to the place, but actually, they cannot afford the ones which have already had work done. So be honest with yourself, what you want, what you can do and what you can afford. I would say see all properties that fit your other criteria, and if one happens to need work don't be afraid, as the location is more important than the decoration. Only if your circumstances mean you absolutely cannot ever get the building work done should you eliminate these from your search.

See below Chapter 11 on buying a property for development.

1.8 New builds

Some people only want a new build property, and are prepared to pay over the odds for a shiny, new finish once building work has completed and the building risks have disappeared. New builds are increasingly popular, and there may be some Government funding available to assist in their purchase. (See Chapter 5 below)

**The Expert's Guide to Buying a House in the UK:
helping you to buy a good home and a good property investment.
by Dr Judith Summer.**

There are even specialist websites to search for new builds such as http://www.smartnewhomes.com/.

It is possible to buy new builds at a discount, either at the end of the project if the developer finds that he has too many empty units and needs to sell quickly to maintain liquidity, or at the beginning of the project when you are buying speculatively "off plan" before building has been completed, (or sometimes before it has even begun) and the developer needs your funds and commitment. However there are risks with such speculation. It is always dangerous to assume that property prices will rise, and you will need to have done your homework to outwit the developer.

When buying offplan you need to know exactly what you will be getting, down to the details of whether the grass will be turfed and whether parking spaces are allocated. If you request certain things at an early enough stage in the build, like colour schemes or finishes, the builder might well agree. Bear in mind that the plot you buy might be in a different location to the show home, with different light and noise levels, and might look a lot more cramped with your own furniture compared to the skeleton furniture in the showroom. You might want to know how many other plots have been sold and whether to people who are going to live there themselves or to buy to let investors, and when completion of all the plots will be. Else you might be the only resident of a large building site for a very long time!

New build purchases carry a risk that the builder will become insolvent before the build is complete, but after you have committed to the purchase. For that reason, you should check that the builder is part of a warranty scheme such as NHBC, Premier Guarantee or LABC Warranty. These schemes should also ensure that your home is built to agreed standards. If the builder is offering a warranty, he will also have to adhere to the Consumer Code for Home Builders. One of its protections is provision that the builder has to refund your money and any fees in full if there is an unreasonable delay (as defined) to the completion date stated in your Contract of Sale.

As mortgage offers have an expiry date, it is sensible not to change jobs before the build is complete in case your mortgage application has to be renewed.

Simma Properties - Finding your little property treasure
Copyright © 2016 Judith Penina Summer
All rights reserved.

The Expert's Guide to Buying a House in the UK:
helping you to buy a good home and a good property investment.
by Dr Judith Summer.

There are pros and cons of buying a new build, and the purchase can be risky and speculative especially towards the beginning of the project, but if that is what you have set your heart upon, then at least be informed of the risks.

1.9 Investment value

When you are buying your home, should you be looking at its future investment value? The answer is both yes and no. If it is going to be your home, the most important thing is that you will be happy living in it day to day and that you can afford to buy it and live there. Having said that, you cannot put your head in the sand and totally ignore any thoughts of its future investment value. It would be silly to buy something which you thought would be worth less in the future, for instance if you knew about a future local development that you thought would reduce its value, such as the building of a new nuclear plant, unless there was some big reason why you needed to be in that location anyway, such as having to live near a sick relative. Similarly, if the exact location of your home is not so important to you as long as it fulfils certain criteria, then it would be worthwhile buying a home in an area where you thought prices were likely to increase, such as near the new Crossrail stations. Areas with amenities like good parks and schools are likely to hold their value more than areas without, and bounce back better from any property market dips such as those which occurred after the UK financial crisis of 2008.

Other than for obvious examples like these, it can be hard to predict future property values. For that reason, I would not try to speculate too much and would concentrate on acquiring the nicest home you can possibly afford to buy that fulfils as many points on your wishlist as possible, and at the right price. If you choose wisely and value the property well, (other chapters in this book can help you to do this), then you should have a good home which also translates into a good investment. Such a home has the greatest chance of withstanding and recovering from the market downturns that do and can happen.

The Expert's Guide to Buying a House in the UK:
helping you to buy a good home and a good property investment.
by Dr Judith Summer.

1.10   Summary top tips

You will need to like your new house or flat, so hopefully it will contain the most important elements of your wishlist to make the nicest home you can possibly afford. Location is going to be key both to your life and to the property's future value. But the potential of a place may be more important that its current state.

The Expert's Guide to Buying a House in the UK:
helping you to buy a good home and a good property investment.
by Dr Judith Summer.

Chapter 2

How do you find properties?

2.1   Online search

2.2   Register with agents

2.3   How estate agents work

2.4   Be proactive

2.5   Viewings

2.6   Buying agents

2.7   Auctions

2.8   Summary top tips

2.1   Online search

Once you have decided on the sort of thing you want, you should look at an online search site. There are many out there, so do not drive yourself mad by feeling you need to look on every one - a couple of the main ones will do! Rightmove is the most popular property search engine, and Zoopla and Prime Location are popular too. Nestoria uses a simple search layout and pulls in information from other property search engines. Gumtree also lists properties for sale, but not so many, and I have never used it to look for property for purchase.

**The Expert's Guide to Buying a House in the UK:
helping you to buy a good home and a good property investment.
by Dr Judith Summer.**

You can also programme the online search site to notify you if other properties crop up which match your search criteria. But there are many properties which never need to make it to these online sites, as they are sold by the agents either off market or so quickly that they are never listed online. That is a big reason why you should register with appropriate agents too.

http://www.smartnewhomes.com/ allows you to search for new builds.

https://propertytorenovate.co.uk/ allows you to search for renovation, auction, derelict and repossessed property, land and building plots.

2.2   Register with agents

Your online search will show you which agents are popping up the most for the sort of properties you are looking for, and these are the ones you should register with. You must register with all the local agents who are selling your sort of property. Telephone any agent who you find is showing a property which is of interest to you. Do not just register with one agent, and assume that he will just do the finding work for you. Most people do not realise that the world of estate agents does not work like that.

2.3   How estate agents work

Most estate agents have a certain number of properties on their books. They get paid if they sell those properties. So those are the ones that they are going to try to sell to you. Sometimes they are offered a fee if they can sell someone else's property, but many agents are not interested in those fees either, as the fee will not be as much, and those properties are competition for the ones on their books. So if one agent happens to be selling your dream house, and you are registered with that one agent, then you have a chance of viewing that house. But if not, you are going to miss out on your dream house.

Do not worry that you are going to offend one agent if you register with other agents. You are expected to register elsewhere as well. The agent works for the seller and is

Simma Properties - Finding your little property treasure
Copyright © 2016 Judith Penina Summer
All rights reserved.

**The Expert's Guide to Buying a House in the UK:
helping you to buy a good home and a good property investment.
by Dr Judith Summer.**

---

paid commission by the seller. He will only be offended if you see a property with another agent when the property is also on his books in a joint agency situation. The agent that gets a fee is the one who first shows you a property. If there is a joint or multiple agency, the agents have agreements between them as to how to split the commission. None of that is the buyer's concern.

2.4   Be proactive

Once you have registered with the agents, you also need to be a bit proactive. Keep an eye out for properties that interest you. Have an alert set up so that anything new which comes to the market and which fits your criteria is sent by the online sites to your email. Tell the agents very carefully the sort of thing you are looking for and which ones you have seen seem to fit the bill.

If you have not heard from an agent for a while, give them a call. Without making yourself a pain, make sure they know who you are, what you want and that you are a serious buyer. Because you want them to call you when a property comes up which is not yet being publicly marketed, and you want to be at the top of the list of people they call. Some of the very best properties are sold before they even get to the online sites, so do not underestimate the importance of frequent and personal contact with the agents in the area.

2.5   Viewings

You do not have to view all the properties which an agent might suggest. Again, he is trying to sell to you and it may be in his interests to persuade you to view everything. If you know you really do not want something, then do not waste your time going to view it. On the other hand, see enough to know whether the agent will be wasting your time or not. It may be a bad idea to judge a property by the style of its outside, as the inside might be spectacular and you will see the inside more often than the outside!

2.6 Buying agents

Some estate agents will act as a buying agent for you if you want them to find a property for you whether or not the property is registered with them. They will charge an extra fee for this which you will have to pay. This might be something like 2.5% of the purchase price. If you are lacking time to do the proper research, this might be a sensible option for you, but bear in mind that the agent might still prefer to sell to you from the properties on his books.

You may prefer to hire a property finder who is independent. For anyone interested, I offer this service too, although I, and any other reputable property finder, will only search in areas in which I am very familiar. Your independent agent should have enough knowledge to be able to tell you which are the good properties down to the road and block.

2.7 Auctions

Auctions are not for the faint-hearted! I would not recommend them unless the buyer is particularly savvy about property values. The trick is to know how much a property is worth and not to bid beyond that number. Although it is possible to pick up a bargain at auction, very often the opposite is true. There is often a reason why a property is offered at auction and not sold in the usual way by estate agents. Sometimes the reason is that there is something peculiar or difficult about the property, such as tenants who will not leave. But the reason is often that the seller thinks he will get a better price at auction. A whole book could be written about auctions and how to deal with them, and this book is not it. If you are set on buying at auction, the website Property Auctions is a database of properties available at auction, with guide prices, results and facilities to request a catalogue.

2.8 Summary top tips

It will be important to register with all the major local estate agents, as well as keeping a close eye on online property search sites. Your relationship with the estate agents should be proactive, but you do not have to view every property they suggest.

The Expert's Guide to Buying a House in the UK:
helping you to buy a good home and a good property investment.
by Dr Judith Summer.

Finding a suitable property can take a lot of time and energy and you will probably need to set significant time aside to do this. If you cannot do this, and you do not mind paying a fee, it may be worth employing a property finder if you want someone independent to do this for you. I appreciate that being a property finder myself, that will sound like biased advice! All I can say is that the property finder is likely to know of off-market and new-to-the-market opportunities before you.

The Expert's Guide to Buying a House in the UK:
helping you to buy a good home and a good property investment.
by Dr Judith Summer.

Chapter 3

How do you work out the value of the property?

3.1 **Three choices**

3.2 **Research sold prices**

3.3 **Price per square foot**

3.4 **Summary top tips**

3.1 Three choices

Once you have found the place you want to buy, how do you work out how much it is worth? You have three choices:

1. you can rely on the estate agent (who acts as agent for the seller and is paid by the seller, not you) to guide you as to the appropriate price. Good luck with that one!

2. you can employ someone independent, who knows the area, to give you a view. But this will cost you. Or

3. you can research the area yourself.

Nowadays with online searches freely available, this is not so daunting a task.

The Expert's Guide to Buying a House in the UK:
helping you to buy a good home and a good property investment.
by Dr Judith Summer.

3.2 Research sold prices

Choose one of the reputable online search sites and look for properties which match your requirements. So if you are looking at a two bed flat with a balcony and parking, search for two bed flats with a balcony and parking. You will have probably done some earlier searches in order to find the properties in the first place.

But this time, you should be looking at the SOLD prices sections of the websites like http://www.rightmove.co.uk/house-prices.html or the Land Registry website from where much of the information is taken. http://nethouseprices.com/ is a website which specialises in providing sold property prices in England and Wales and where possible, it shows the estate agents who have sold the properties, images, the number of bedrooms and floorplans with square footage, so you can work out the sold price per square foot (see below). https://www.propertypriceadvice.co.uk/ is another sold house price site and also has an easy to use free valuation tool, although I am not sure how accurate the tool is. https://www.ros.gov.uk/property-data/house-price-search is probably the site to use for Scotland's sold house prices. Please bear in mind that sometimes information on these sites is not complete or up to date, and there may be errors.

It is all very well to know that there are a number of properties out there that match the asking price of the property you are looking at, but the asking prices may be unrealistic, especially if the property has been sitting there a while. So you need to know what equivalent properties have sold for over approximately the last year or 18/24 months or so. That should tell you what the market value is and any patterns. The market has spoken! Be patient, as it can take quite a while to go through the data.

The sale talk of an estate agent may include information about how much the price has been discounted, so what a bargain you are getting. If the property did not sell at the higher price, then the higher price was probably not the true market price and should be largely ignored. Sale banter is just that. It is no different to sale banter in a shop. The local sold prices are what will guide you to the market value of a property.

The Expert's Guide to Buying a House in the UK:
helping you to buy a good home and a good property investment.
by Dr Judith Summer.

3.3 Price per square foot

An excellent indicator of value is how much equivalent properties have sold worked out on a price per square foot basis. You can then quite easily compare the price that the property you like is being offered at against equivalent ones that have sold recently. That is how most of those in the business value property, especially in urban areas where there are lots of similar properties around.

In case anyone is too embarrassed to ask how to do this calculation or find this information out, this is how. On the plan which the estate agents have done, the total square footage is usually marked. Divide the sold price by the total square footage.

Price per square foot = (Price of property) divided by (Total square footage)

Then apply the price per square foot which you find on average, to the property you are looking at. You do this by multiplying the price per square foot by the total square foot of the property you are looking at.

The price the property is worth = (Average price per square foot) multiplied by (Total square footage of the property you are looking at)

You can adapt the figure to take into account the condition and facilities on offer. So add a bit more to the figure per square foot if the property has extra facilities to the average one, like a private balcony on a flat, or parking for two cars in a driveway for a house. Take off the cost of refurbishment if the property you are looking at needs refurbishment.

Bear in mind that this formula method should help you to value property, but property valuation is still an art, not a science that will necessarily fit a formula. Sometimes familiarity and experience with the area are needed to give you a feel for how the figure should be adapted. Sometimes you may be able to ask a friendly estate agent in the area who is not selling you this particular property, but I would beware of giving them the address of the actual property you are looking at with their rival.

The Expert's Guide to Buying a House in the UK:
helping you to buy a good home and a good property investment.
by Dr Judith Summer.

3.4 Summary top tips

Look for the sold prices of similar properties to establish the market price and apply the price per square foot. Use a calculator and check your numbers- there is no point getting important figures incorrect due to errors in mental arithmetic! You will then need to assess the cost of what you want against the cost of what you can afford.

The Expert's Guide to Buying a House in the UK:
helping you to buy a good home and a good property investment.
by Dr Judith Summer.

Chapter 4

Affordability and buying costs

4.1 Youth, prospects and payment protection insurance

4.2 Spending versus earnings: how much is left over?

4.3 Level of mortgage

4.4 Deposit

4.5 Extra buying costs

4.5.1 Stamp duty in the UK

4.5.2 Your solicitors' fees and expenses

4.5.3 Buildings insurance (for a house)

4.5.4 Mortgage fees

4.5.5 House building surveys

4.5.6 Removal costs

4.5.7 Any repairs/ refurbishment

4.5.8 Post redirection

4.5.9 The costs of running a home

4.6 Summary top tips

The Expert's Guide to Buying a House in the UK:
helping you to buy a good home and a good property investment.
by Dr Judith Summer.

I keep mentioning affordability. The reality is that you can only safely buy what you can afford.

4.1 Youth, prospects and payment protection insurance

When my husband and I were both young and employed in excellent professional jobs with good prospects, we were advised to borrow as much as we could afford. We did and that advice paid off for us. But we were prepared to make sacrifices and live within a budget. The reality of a mortgage which eats up a lot of your income is that you may have to accept that you might not be able to afford the lifestyle you had before. Take-aways, frequent nights out, designer clothes etc may all have to be sacrificed, although perhaps they are already being sacrificed to rent and student loan repayments.

Life insurance and payment protection insurance may be something that you will want to consider over and above the insurance which may be part of your job's benefit package, to ensure that your mortgage will get paid in the case of death or incapacity. This book is not the place to discuss the ins and outs of taking out such policies and I would advise that you obtain professional, independent advice if you think this is of interest to you, although such policies will add to your monthly living expenses.

4.2 Spending versus earnings: how much is left over?

Whatever the case, you need realistically to assess how much you tend to spend every year so you can assess how much you might need next year and put this against earnings after tax.

A rough and ready way of doing this is looking at your current account/s overall spend in a year, assuming that credit card bills are paid from this account. Deduct from this amount the current housing costs you are spending, whether it is rent or mortgage. This gives you a rough idea of what you have spent in the last year aside from housing costs. You can do this exercise for as many years as makes you feel comfortable.

The Expert's Guide to Buying a House in the UK:
helping you to buy a good home and a good property investment.
by Dr Judith Summer.

To work out what you might need to spend in the future, you may need to add increased expenses if you are going to try to buy a bigger property, including council tax, water, electric, gas and insurance. Add in any extra expenditures that you know you are going to have to incur in the next year which you were not already incurring eg childcare costs or school fees.

Whatever figure you come to, you then need to take it away from your current net wage or wages and you should hopefully end up with an amount left over which could be spent yearly on a new mortgage.

A mortgage company uses similar affordability calculations to help them decide what they will lend you, and will want to know about your income and outgoings.

4.3   Level of mortgage

You then need to find out what sum you could borrow which would result in yearly payments equal to or less than the amount you have left over after your yearly expenses. It is easiest to find this out by asking a mortgage broker. There are also online mortgage calculators.

But it is not over yet, as you need to have enough left over if the mortgage interest rate was not the current rate, but increased say by at least 5 extra points.

Mortgage companies typically loan between 3 and 5 times the combined income of the applicant or applicants. And they will tell you what proportion of the property price they will lend to you. This is called the LTV or loan to value. Usually, the smaller the loan is in relation to the value of the whole property, the lower the interest rate will be.

4.4   Deposit

You will need to have some savings for a deposit too, ie the amount that the bank is not lending you to buy the property. Although there are some UK government help schemes available for certain new homes and for some first time buyers which mean

**The Expert's Guide to Buying a House in the UK:
helping you to buy a good home and a good property investment.
by Dr Judith Summer.**

---

only a 5% deposit is needed, other purchases will require much more of a deposit, often 25%. Brief details of some of the government schemes available can be found in the next chapter on Mortgages.

4.5   Extra buying costs

There are more costs involved in buying a property than just its price, including the following for which you will have to make provision.

4.5.1 Stamp duty in the UK.

You have to have this money available at the date of completion and you cannot borrow it. The amount of stamp duty payable can be substantial and is worked out on a rising scale depending on the amount of the purchase price.

0% for purchases up to £125,000
2% for the part of the purchase £125,001 to £250,000
5% for the part of the purchase £250,001 to £925,000
10% for the part of the purchase £925,001 to £1,500,000
12% for the part of the purchase over £1,500,000

Rather than try to work it out, it is easier to type the appropriate purchase price into an online stamp duty calculator such as: http://www.hmrc.gov.uk/tools/sdlt/land-and-property.htm

Changes from 4th December 2014 mean that people who buy homes under £937,000 will pay less stamp duty than under the previous system, but the sums can still be large. After 1st April 2016, those buying a second home or buy to let property over £40,000 will have an additional 3% stamp duty to pay.

The Expert's Guide to Buying a House in the UK:
helping you to buy a good home and a good property investment.
by Dr Judith Summer.

4.5.2 Your solicitors' fees and expenses

You have to pay your solicitors' fees and expenses for carrying out the purchase for you, plus VAT as applicable. You have to use a solicitor or licensed conveyancer: this is not something you can just do yourself unless you are qualified, and the mortgage companies tend not to allow you to do your own conveyancing even if you are qualified. The expenses will include money for the land searches your solicitors will have to carry out to check certain things about the property you wish to purchase, plus compulsory land registration fees after the purchase so that your purchase is logged at the Land Registry.

Depending on the mortgage deal offered by your mortgage company, you may also have to pay solicitors' fees incurred by the mortgage company who will want the same checks carried out to show that the property is worthy of their investment. If your solicitor is on the panel of the mortgage company, this should condense the costs together. However, if your solicitor is not on the panel of the mortgage company, you may have to pay all the fees of the mortgage company's solicitor in addition to those of your solicitor.

Your solicitor will tell you in advance how much the expected fees will be. Some firms will offer a fixed fee for the whole conveyance, and some will offer a rate per hour, usually with a maximum fee. It is advisable to shop around on fees, but if you know someone is recommended, it may be very worthwhile going with that recommendation, as sometimes you get what you pay for.

Which? April 2016 suggests that all fees and expenses might be up to £1,500 for a property worth over £500,000, about £1,250 for properties worth £250,000 to £300,000 and over £1,000 for a property worth £100,000 to £250,000. In London you can find fees much higher than this, especially if you look at a West End or City firm and especially if the property in question is worth a lot more. Depending on what you have agreed with your solicitor, you will usually be liable for their costs and expenses incurred even if the purchase falls through.

4.5.3 Buildings insurance (for a house)

If you are getting a mortgage on a house, the mortgage company will usually require you also to obtain buildings insurance, so this is not something you can just skip. Depending on the contract of sale and the terms of the mortgage, you may have to have this in place from exchange of contracts, not just at completion of the purchase. Either way, I would suggest that you arrange this early so the insurance is available at the drop of a hat, the moment you ring and tell the insurer that your contract has exchanged. I have known some purchases which were delayed because there was a problem getting insurance for the property, and the buyer nearly lost out.

It is fairly easy nowadays to obtain quotations online or through a broker. There are also specialist insurers for "difficult" properties, for instance if there are signs of subsidence or if the house is going to be unoccupied for a period of time. One tip I have discovered: it is hard to find an insurer for a property which is both suffering from subsidence and is going to be unoccupied. You may have to occupy a property after completion which might be suffering from subsidence in order to get insurance.

And don't forget, you might want contents insurance as well, and there are advantages to getting contents insurance with the same insurer as the buildings insurer. For instance, if there were ever a dispute between a contents and a buildings insurer as to who was responsible for particular damage, that conflict would fall away if they were the same insurer.

4.5.4 Mortgage fees

Often the mortgage company will pay a mortgage broker's fee, but you may still have to pay other mortgage fees, including arrangement fees and property valuation fees. Sometimes these fees can be accumulated into the loan, on top of the amount you are asking to borrow, and you will have to pay interest on this sum in addition to the interest on the loan. Sometimes the mortgage company will not charge actual fees, but instead the interest rate may be a lot higher. The mortgage company will want its own property valuation carried out, incurring a fee, whatever survey of the property you choose to have done, although sometimes the fees can be minimised where the same

**The Expert's Guide to Buying a House in the UK:
helping you to buy a good home and a good property investment.
by Dr Judith Summer.**

---

person is appointed by both you and your mortgage company to carry out your respective surveys.

How much might you have to spend on mortgage valuations? The amount will vary according to the value of the property. Figures from Which? April 2016 show that it might be £290 for a property worth £100,000 to £250,000; £400 for a property worth £400-450,000; and £575 for a property worth over £500,000.

How much might you have to spend on mortgage arrangement fees? Which? April 2016 figures show arrangement fees varying again in line with the value of the property, with fees of £350 for a property worth £100,000 to £250,00; £1,000 for a property worth £400-450,000; and £1,500 for a property worth over £500,000.

4.5.5 House building surveys

The valuation survey carried out by the mortgage company simply tells the mortgage company whether the property is worth enough for them to lend money to you. It does not look at the structure of the property, so will not be able to highlight any problems there might be. This is one reason why you should take out your own survey of the property. (The position is different in Scotland, where the seller has a duty to provide a Home Report pack within 9 days of marketing a property, and this must include a survey and property valuation, although sometimes it is advisable to get your own anyway in addition.) The principle of caveat emptor (buyer beware) still very much applies, which means that you buy the property as you find it, in whatever condition it is, and it is up to you to find out what that condition is.

If you find out in advance of exchange that there are problems with the property you wish to purchase, that may mean that you can ask the seller to put it right, or negotiate on the purchase price to take account of the work that will need to be done to deal with any problem found by the surveyor. If the surveyor does not spot a serious problem he should have spotted which has serious consequences, it may possible to hold him responsible at a later date for the costs of putting things right (Legal advice may have to be taken in such a case). It is unlikely that you will be able to rely in a legal sense on the mortgage company's valuation, as that is carried out on behalf of the mortgage company rather than on behalf of you.

**The Expert's Guide to Buying a House in the UK:
helping you to buy a good home and a good property investment.
by Dr Judith Summer.**

There are two main types of survey, a homebuyer's report and a building survey. A condition report is less detailed than either of these. A fourth type of survey is a snagging survey for a new build. Whatever type of survey you may decide to obtain, it is important to use a reputable and suitable qualified surveyor who is a member of RICS.

(a) Condition report

This is a basic report which might be suitable for newer homes in good condition. It only gives a broad-brush approach, highlighting things like whether there is a gas and water supply, whether there is a garage or other outbuildings and providing a summary of issues and risks for your solicitor to look into, such as evidence of bad electrics, ownership of boundaries and planning permission for extensions or other building work. The survey will be limited to what the surveyor can see: he will not be lifting up floor boards or moving furniture. Which? April 2016 estimates this might cost £150- £300. I would usually personally err on the side of caution and get a more detailed report than this.

(b) Homebuyer's report

This covers the general condition of the property and may be adequate for conventional properties less than 40 years old which are in a reasonable condition. The report will also include a property valuation (usually at a relatively small additional cost), which the more detailed building survey will not do, although it is expected from summer 2016 that you will be able to opt out of the property valuation part.

The report should include what would be included in the condition report. As for the condition report, a Homebuyer's report will only include what the surveyor can see and so again he will not be lifting floorboards or moving furniture. In addition, the report should include:

- an insurance reinstatement figure. This is not the same as a valuation which would be the total value of the land plus the building on top of it which together comprise the property as a whole. Instead, this is an estimate of the cost of the building itself,

**The Expert's Guide to Buying a House in the UK:
helping you to buy a good home and a good property investment.
by Dr Judith Summer.**

---

and so of how much the property would need to be insured for in case it burnt down and needed to be reinstated.

- a clear summary of problems which might make a difference to the property's value.

- advice on any repairs or maintenance that need to be done to the property.

- any issues which require closer attention to avoid serious damage or dangerous conditions.

- general information about the area, environment and energy efficiency.

- any legal considerations.

The costs of a survey vary according to the value of the property. Which? April 2016 say that a Homebuyer's report might cost £500 for a property worth £100,000 to £250,000; £700 for a property worth £350,000 to £500,000; and £950 for a property worth over £500,000.

(c) Building survey

This is a far more detailed survey, and used to be called a structural survey. It is the most expensive and time consuming type of survey, and it may take a week or two before the survey is ready. By comparison the other surveys can usually be done and sent to you within a couple of days. Bear the time in mind if you are under a tight or competitive deadline to exchange contracts on a purchase.

Although it is more costly, the cost is not necessarily so much more than a Homebuyer's report, and depending on the size of the purchase, the extra money may be worth spending against the risk of not discovering a major defect. I would definitely recommend a full Building Survey if the property is large, old, listed, dilapidated, has a thatched roof or timber frame, or has an unusual structure (such as if it is an old windmill). However, it might not be worth doing if you were planning to strip the property on purchase, do some structural work to the whole thing, (for instance if you intended to build a basement) and carry out a total refurbishment.

**The Expert's Guide to Buying a House in the UK:
helping you to buy a good home and a good property investment.
by Dr Judith Summer.**

For a full Building Survey, Which? April 2016 say the cost might be £700 for a property worth £100,000 to £250,000; £900 for a property worth £350,000 to £500,000; and £1300 for a property worth over £500,000.

The Building Survey, in addition to all the features of a Homebuyer Report, will include:

- a thorough inspection and report.

- summary of defects, both significant and insignificant.

- potential problems caused by hidden flaws.

- advice on repair options, their estimated cost and any consequences of failing to address them.

- advice and considerations for your solicitor.

(d) Snagging survey

If you are buying a new-build home which typically comes with a 10 year NHBC building guarantee, you may not need a full building survey. You may wish to get a snagging survey which checks the property for defects and poor finishes such as bad paintwork or crooked guttering. Which? April 2016 estimates the costs of one of these might be £300 to £600.

4.5.6 Removal costs

You may have no worldly goods other than your clothes and a few boxes of books, all of which fit into the boot of a car. But obviously, your moving costs will be greater if you are moving with a whole family with a whole family's worth of things. It is useful to get quite a few quotations for moving costs. You can compare quotations from well-known names, recommendations from friends and random online sites. Packing costs are extra, but may not be so very much more. I have found that there are super expensive, well-known brands of removal companies, very cheap man-with-a-van

**The Expert's Guide to Buying a House in the UK:
helping you to buy a good home and a good property investment.
by Dr Judith Summer.**

---

options and something in between, and that again you probably pay for the level of professionalism you get. Some firms offer unpacking services too, so what you spend on moving costs may vary greatly and will depend on your circumstances.

Which? April 2016 has looked into these costs. On average, hiring a van might cost £100 for a one bedroom flat or £200 for a two bedroom flat. Which? does not recommend hiring a van for bigger properties. Removal companies can be £400 for a one bedroom, £500 for a two bedroom, £800 for a three bedroom and £1,000 for a four bedroom. Packing costs in addition could be between £150 for a one bedroom to £350 for a four bedroom.

4.5.7 Any repairs/ refurbishment

Unless it is a new build, you will probably end up wanting to do more to a new purchase than you think you will at first! If you are lucky, you may not have to do any work right away and this may instead be something you can save for.

4.5.8 Post redirection

This will seem like a small cost in the scheme of things, but it all adds up. Currently in 2016 Post Office redirection in the UK costs per last name £31.99 for up to 3 months, £41.99 for up to 6 months and £59.99 for up to 12 months.

4.5.9 The costs of running a home

The costs of running a home will be something else to factor in, especially if this is a first time purchase or a step up the ladder. There will be bills such as for gas, electric, telephone, broadband, TV licence, insurance, parking, service charges, ground rents and Council tax.

4.6 Summary top tips

Carefully work out what you can afford before you jump into the buying process, and bear in mind the costs over and above the purchase price. Spend your youth saving as much money as you can. Do not commit to a purchase that you know you cannot afford. You may have to adjust your property aspirations according to what you can afford, but don't give up hope that one day you may be able to afford exactly what you want. You can still make a good purchase even if it is not your ideal. And of course, a home is what you make of it, not just the bricks and mortar.

Chapter 5

Mortgages

5.1   Mortgage in principle

5.2   Process and terms

5.3   Independent mortgage brokers

5.4   Mortgage fees

5.5   Speed

5.6   Buy to let mortgages

5.7   Government help schemes

5.7.1   Help to Buy

(a) Help to Buy equity loan

(b) Help to Buy London

(c) Help to Buy Mortgage Guarantee

(d) Forces Help to Buy

5.7.2   Starter Homes

5.7.3   Shared Ownership

5.7.4   First Time Buyer's Initiative

The Expert's Guide to Buying a House in the UK:
helping you to buy a good home and a good property investment.
by Dr Judith Summer.

5.7.5 Help to Buy ISA

5.7.6 Lifetime ISA

5.7.7 Right to Buy Scheme

5.8 The Bank of Mum and Dad

5.9 Summary top tips

5.1 Mortgage in principle

If you need a mortgage you should always apply in plenty of time. Even before you have found a property, you should try to obtain a mortgage in principle, which means that a particular mortgage provider has approved you based on your savings, earnings and projected expenditure for a mortgage up to a certain amount, at a certain rate if you pay a certain amount of deposit. It will be easier to move quickly on a purchase if a mortgage in principle is in place, and it will make you a more attractive bidder than someone who does not have one. A mortgage in principle will usually have an expiry date.

Having a mortgage in principle means that a mortgage offer being forthcoming will only depend on the mortgage valuation of the property you wish to buy supporting the amount you want to borrow. So the valuer basically has to say that there is enough equity or value in the property for it to be held as collateral for the loan..

5.2 Process and terms

The mortgage provider has to approve both you and the property you wish to buy before it will issue a mortgage offer. The offer will say when it will expire. This means that you will need to complete the purchase before the expiry date else the mortgage provider may not provide the loan. If the timing is an issue, you need to get

on to the mortgage company and get them either to extend the time limit or renew the offer.

Every mortgage provider will have its own criteria for a loan, requiring the applicant to provide a certain percentage of the purchase price and requiring a particular loan to value ratio (ie the amount the bank is prepared to lend as a percentage of how much the property is worth). Buy to let mortgage providers will also be concerned about the yield, ie how much rent can be achieved on the property as a percentage of the value of the property.

Mortgage companies will want to see a written application with documents in support, such as payslips and bank account statements. Omitting even one document can cause huge delays. Nowadays, mortgage companies may wish to interview applicants as well as review their paper application.

Once you have applied for a mortgage and received a mortgage offer, your solicitor should handle the process of actually getting the money from the mortgage company to the seller as part of the conveyancing. Your solicitor will need to see a copy of the mortgage offer and may need to liaise with the mortgage provider's solicitor if he is not acting for both you and the mortgage company. If you are not sure what is happening, feel free to ask until you are absolutely clear and are sure that you solicitor is in fact dealing with this part of the process. Your solicitor should ask for the money from the mortgage company so it arrives into your solicitor's account when it is supposed to, in readiness for completion. It will not be available to you until completion, so make sure you have enough cash to pay the amount required on exchange of contracts, which is usually 10% of the purchase price, but a different figure can be negotiated.

5.3   Independent mortgage brokers

It is a good idea to appoint an independent mortgage broker. Check who is paying their fees. Usually in the UK it will be the bank or building society from which you borrow, so it actually costs you nothing to get expert advice from an expert in the field, who has access to more information than you can possibly hope to obtain, and saving you hours of work trolling through data to find a good mortgage product.

The Expert's Guide to Buying a House in the UK:
helping you to buy a good home and a good property investment.
by Dr Judith Summer.

The better brokers will liaise with the bank or building society so as to establish exactly what information and documentation is required, request this from you, fill out the forms for you and send off the application with everything required attached. They can liaise during the mortgage application process and chase the bank or building society as necessary too, and may have contacts and relationships with the people involved which can only help.

If a mortgage adviser is sitting in the office of a high street bank or building society, then he is unlikely to be an independent adviser, and will probably be tied to offering only the products that are offered by that bank or building society.

It is worth asking your friends and family if they recommend any particular broker. Some estate agents may also suggest brokers, although that is not necessarily the same as a recommendation, especially if the estate agent is receiving some sort of referral commission.

5.4   Mortgage fees

As mentioned above at paragraph 5.5.4, you usually have to pay for the fees of the mortgage company, which will include their solicitor's fees if your solicitor is not on their panel. You will also have to pay for the mortgage valuation survey, and there may be an application fee too, although you may be able to add these on to the loan. Remember, the mortgage surveyor is usually working for the mortgage company, not you, and a mortgage valuation survey is not the same as a housebuyer's full building survey.

If you are not clear about what fees you are going to pay, please ask the broker or mortgage provider, although the fees are usually set out clearly in the documentation provided to you.

5.5 Speed

If you need a mortgage, it will slow the whole purchase down, so be as prepared as you can, and respond by return to any requests from the mortgage company for information or documentation. It is a good idea to ask, before you commit to a timing for an exchange of contracts on the conveyancing, how long the mortgage provider anticipates it will take to provide a mortgage offer. Keep the estate agent up to date with information if there are any delays. He is probably the one who can persuade the seller to stick with you in cases of delay and not to re-market the property or send sale papers out to another buyer.

5.6 Buy to let mortgages

Buy to let mortgages usually have a more expensive interest rate than homeowners' mortgages. Homeowners without a buy to let mortgage are meant to notify and obtain approval of their bank or building society if they wish to let out their property. Then the bank or building society may increase the interest rate. If no notification is made, and the bank finds out, there may be consequences as set out in the terms of the mortgage deed. The bank's criteria for lending is different if the mortgage is buy to let, rather than own home. For instance, buy to let products will be looking not only at the value of the property against the amount of the loan (the loan to value ratio), but also the yield (per cent that the rent has against the value of the property) having a certain minimum to support the repayments.

5.7 Government help schemes

At the time of writing in 2016, these are some of the special mortgages and savings available, but please check out all details carefully yourself and do not rely on this brief summary which is provided for information only. More details should be available online, and the schemes may change over time, or more schemes may become available. Just look at the details carefully and make sure you are not paying a huge amount of interest, on a huge percentage of the purchase price.

The Expert's Guide to Buying a House in the UK:
helping you to buy a good home and a good property investment.
by Dr Judith Summer.

5.7.1 Help to Buy

- not to be used in conjunction with any other Government scheme such as Right to Buy or Shared Ownership.

- only for first or only homes.

- not to be let out.

There are three types of Help to Buy schemes:

(a) Help to Buy equity loan

- For first-time buyers and home movers who are buying a new build home, probably up to 2021.

- For homes up to a value of £600,000.

- Buyer provides at least 5% deposit.

- The Government to provide a loan up to 20% of the property value; interest free for the first 5 years; after that interest at 1.75% ; loan to be repaid after 25 years or on sale if that happens first.

- A lender participating in the scheme provides a loan for the remaining 75% of the property value.

(b) Help to Buy London

- The same features as Help to Buy equity loan, but if the property is in London, the Government will provide up to 40% of the property value.

- The buyer still provides 5% deposit and the participating lender provides the rest.

Simma Properties - Finding your little property treasure
Copyright © 2016 Judith Penina Summer
All rights reserved.

**The Expert's Guide to Buying a House in the UK:
helping you to buy a good home and a good property investment.
by Dr Judith Summer.**

(c) Help to Buy Mortgage Guarantee

- For new build or already existing homes.

- The buyer does not have to be a first time buyer.

- For homes up to a value of £600,000.

- Buyer provides at least 5% deposit. (Actually, 5% to 20%)

- Government offers the mortgage lender a guarantee of a further 15% of the property's value if the buyer defaults.

- Buyer takes out a mortgage for the remainder of the purchase price.

- This scheme is due to end on 31 December 2016. (ie completions by this date).

(d) Forces Help to Buy

- Eligible servicemen and servicewomen can borrow up to 50% of their salary interest free for a deposit and buying costs such as legal fees.

- The maximum loan is £25,000, to be repaid over 10 years.

5.7.2 Starter Homes

- A limited number of new homes will be offered at a 20% discount to those registered on the http://www.starter-home.co.uk/ website.

- Only for first time buyers under the age of 40.

5.7.3 Shared Ownership

- For new homes or new homes re-sold by housing associations.

The Expert's Guide to Buying a House in the UK:
helping you to buy a good home and a good property investment.
by Dr Judith Summer.

- For first-time buyers or anyone who has formerly owned a home but cannot afford one now.

- Collective household income £80,000 (or £90,000 in London).

- Buyer purchases just a stake of a new build home from a housing association (between 25% and 75%).

- Buyer provides 10% deposit on the relevant share.

- Buyer pays "affordable" rent to the housing association on the proportion of the home which he does not own.

- Buyer can buy more shares of the property at a later date until he owns it all.

5.7.4 First Time Buyer's Initiative

- Only those who qualify for the scheme can apply, and they are mainly key workers such as those who work in the emergency services, nurses and teachers.

- First time buyers only who can prove that they cannot afford to buy a home that is within travelling distance of their work.

- Household income less than £60,000.

- New builds only.

- Buyer pays for 50% of the cost of the property by a mixture of at least 5% deposit and a mortgage.

- Government pays the other 50% directly to the builder of the new development.

- The Government will be entitled to 50% of the sale value -ie the proportion of their share of the house at the time of the sale.

**The Expert's Guide to Buying a House in the UK:
helping you to buy a good home and a good property investment.
by Dr Judith Summer.**

- After 3 years, buyer will need to pay 1% per year of the amount the Government lent, increasing each year, but will not go higher than 3% after 5 years.

- Buyer can choose to reduce the amount owed to the Government by making repayments on the current market value of the property.

5.7.5 Help to Buy ISA

- For first time buyers

- Government to provide a £50 tax free bonus for every £200 saved each month in a special Help to Buy ISA.

- If balance in the ISA reaches £12,000, the Government bonus will be £3,000, the maximum allowed.

- Funds can be put towards a new build or existing home, so long as the purchase price is not more than £250,000 (or £450,000 in London).

5.7.6 Lifetime ISA

- Available from April 2017.

- For 18-40 year olds - who can save up to £4,000 per year into the account and receive a tax-free Government bonus up to £1,000 per year.

- All or some of the money can go towards a first home at £450,000 or less.

5.7.7 Right to Buy Scheme

-For eligible council and housing association tenants in England, to help them buy their home with a discount of up to £77,900 (or £103,900 in London).

- You have to be a tenant for 3 years before you can buy your home.

5.8 The Bank of Mum and Dad

In this day and age, children often turn to the Bank of Mum and Dad to help them get on to or move up the property ladder. The process is easy if the parents can simply provide extra cash, but there are other options to help offspring, or indeed others, if a cash injection is not possible. It is advisable for such people to take independent financial advice, especially if they are still paying a mortgage on their own home or wish to remortgage their own home to be able to provide cash for others.

Guarantor mortgages mean that the guarantor guarantees to pay any mortgage repayment that the guarantee fails to pay. So if the child defaults, the parent guarantor would have to pay the mortgage instead. The amount that the child can borrow is based on the parents' income and assets as well as theirs.

A parent can take out a joint mortgage with their child, which means that both the parent and the child will be named on the mortgage agreement and on the deeds. Both will be equally liable for repayments, and the property could not be sold without both agreeing. The amount of a joint mortgage would again be based on both the parent's and the child's income, and the bank would bear in mind any money outstanding on the parent's own mortgage. Unfortunately, if the parents already owned their own home, taking out a joint mortgage on another property would count as ownership of a second home and so bring the 3% stamp duty surcharge into play.

5.9 Summary top tips

If you need a mortgage it is a good idea to use an independent mortgage broker, preferably recommended by people you know and trust. Always try to get a mortgage in principle in place as soon as your buying process starts. Consider Government funded options, especially if you are a first time buyer and/or buying a new build, and research thoroughly and independently of this book whether you and/or your proposed purchase will qualify.

The Expert's Guide to Buying a House in the UK:
helping you to buy a good home and a good property investment.
by Dr Judith Summer.

Chapter 6

What to find out from the agent

6.1　Why are they selling?

6.2　Are they motivated to sell?

6.3　Are there any bids on the property.

6.4　The agent cannot lie?

6.5　Summary top tips

I think there are only three main things you should try to find out from the agent in advance of seeing a property and making a bid.

6.1　Why are they selling?

Of course, there will be some moving reasons which should not cause you any concern. Downsizing, upsizing, moving abroad, moving to be near family or near a new job are all reasons for moving which are individual to the seller and do not necessarily show there is a problem with the property.

If there is a problem with the property, it may be hard to get to the bottom of the question which you must pose as to why the property is being sold, and you may have to read between the lines. If the house is not suitable for the seller, it may not be suitable for you. Are they selling because they can't stand the neighbours? You won't like them either, but they are hardly likely to say this straight out. Is the house too small for them now they have children? It might be too small for you if you are

**The Expert's Guide to Buying a House in the UK:
helping you to buy a good home and a good property investment.
by Dr Judith Summer.**

---

thinking of having children soon. If the answer as to why the property is being sold is not straightforward, forthcoming and believable, you may consider investigating matters further, as discussed in Chapter 8.

6.2. Are they motivated to sell?

Does the seller want to sell or are they just seeing what will happen? Do they have somewhere lined up to move to? Are they being forced to sell? This will influence the price. If they are just sitting there waiting for the right price to come along, then it will be harder for you to get it for a good price. If they are trying to exchange on another purchase, they will be motivated to negotiate. If their property has been on the market for a long time, they might also be motivated to negotiate.

6.3. Are there any bids on the property.

Although there is limited information that the agent may be able to give you about other bids, he should tell you if there are others bidding for the place, and if there is other interest. This should inform the level of any offer you may wish to make, including whether it is worth making a low, speculative bid. Of course, if there is more than one agent involved, the one who has shown you the property may not know if there is another bid via another agent, but you can at least ask him to find out.

6.4 The agent cannot lie?

Estate agents are not allowed to lie to you under English law - although I suppose they still might! There are more protections under the new regulations than under the old Property Misdescriptions Act 1991 which was repealed from 1 October 2013, and reliance is now placed on the Consumer Protection from Unfair Trading Regulations 2008 and the Business Protection from Misleading Markets Regulations 2008. If an agent misleads you, he or she could be prosecuted by the local authority trading standards, and it is evidence in a contract avoidance dispute.

The Expert's Guide to Buying a House in the UK:
helping you to buy a good home and a good property investment.
by Dr Judith Summer.

However, caveat emptor still applies, which means that it is up to the buyer to find out what the condition of the property is, as the buyer is buying the property in whatever state it is. Further, you cannot rely on any representations by the seller or the agent unless they are confirmed in writing via the seller's solicitors. For this reason, it is important to tell your solicitor anything that the seller or the agent has represented or promised to you so that he can get this verified in writing.

6.5   Summary top tips

The motivation of the seller will have a huge impact on the price they may be willing to accept. So you should try to find out from the estate agent what the seller's story is as well as the history of the property's current sale and any other bids.

Chapter 7

Top tips when viewing a property

7.1 Your wish list

7.2 See a property you like more than once

7.3 Turn the lights off in the day

7.4 Phone reception

7.5 TV reception

7.6 Water Pressure

7.7 Don't get distracted by the condition of the property, good or bad

7.8 Judge the house on its more permanent characteristics

7.9 Major turn-offs

7.10 Does the survey support your choice?

7.11 Summary top tips

When you view a property, it can be hard to know what you are looking for or how to decide between the properties on offer. These are some tips, in no particular order, to

The Expert's Guide to Buying a House in the UK:
helping you to buy a good home and a good property investment.
by Dr Judith Summer.

---

help you work out which property is right for you and some suggestions of things that you should check out before you make your decision.

7.1   Your wish list

Look to see if a property has the features which you listed as important before you began your search. Write a list of the things you liked about a property and see if it matches your wish list. If you have to choose between two properties you like, which score equally on your checklist, go with your gut!

7.2.   See a property you like more than once

You may think you know on a first viewing if the property is right for you, but go a second time, maybe taking someone else with you. If all is well, your second visit will confirm your view and make you feel more confident in your choice. If you like a property, it is a good idea to see it again at a different time of day - daylight and night time. Look at the light and the environment of the road. Be suspicious if you are told you cannot visit at a different time of day - but there may be a simple reason like a baby's bedtime, although in that case you could still visit the road at night.

7.3   Turn the lights off in the day.

Estate agents often put all the lights on even in the day, so that you will not notice that this is a dark house, or that there is a dark area. I tend to turn the lights off to see what the place looks like in natural light. I don't want to live all my days in an area which has to be artificially lighted, and dark may also mean cold or colder. There are things that can be done to increase daylight, but they may require planning permission or may be physically impossible, and a dark house is not attractive.

Simma Properties - Finding your little property treasure

Copyright © 2016 Judith Penina Summer

All rights reserved.

The Expert's Guide to Buying a House in the UK:
helping you to buy a good home and a good property investment.
by Dr Judith Summer.

7.4   Phone reception

Turn your phone on, try to make a call and try to pick up your email. See if reception in the property is OK, else being stuck not being able to use your mobile in the home may drive you mad. You can also look at websites to check on broadband coverage and how far the exchange is from the property, such as https://www.samknows.com/broadband/broadband_checker or http://labs.thinkbroadband.com/local/index.php?tab=3

7.5   TV reception

Turn on the TV - is the aerial or satellite reception OK? You may not care about television, but if you do, you will want to be able to watch it.

7.6   Water pressure

Turn on the taps - what is the water pressure like? This may only colour your view of what work you may need to do to the property if you buy it, as usually water pressure inside can be increased, but in flats you may not be allowed to add a pump etc.

7.7   Don't get distracted by the condition of the property, good or bad

It is important not to be distracted by the decor, good or bad, or the mess or any funny smell. You may love the job that the professional house dresser has done, but that does not mean you will love the house once that furniture is gone. If it has been professionally dressed, sometimes you are able to buy the furniture with the house, but this does not happen in the majority of sales. You may love the fact that a home is all new and refurbished and feels lovely when you go in, but if it is too small for you, it will still be too small for you! You might like the smell of coffee or fresh bread, but you should wonder if you are being unduly influenced! I once nearly did not buy the home we lived in very happily for 10 years because there was a funny smell which put

**The Expert's Guide to Buying a House in the UK:
helping you to buy a good home and a good property investment.
by Dr Judith Summer.**

---

us off at first. I made a list of all the things I liked and disliked about the property, and the only thing on the dislike list was the smell, so we bought the house and got to the bottom of the smell. Some incense had been burnt to hide the bad smell coming from a leak in the ground floor WC, a leak which was easy to fix. It is very easy to be influenced one way or another by the contents of a home, but walls can be repainted, and furniture, cushions and rugs are moveable.

7.8. Judge the house on its more permanent characteristics

Instead, you should judge the house on its more permanent characteristics. How big are the rooms. What is the total square footage? What is the light like? Are most of the living rooms north facing? Is there a driveway? Is the house or garden overlooked? Is there any room for an extension?

7.9 Major turn-offs

Assuming you can afford otherwise, beware buying properties with a major turn-off. This might include properties with a vent from the London Underground in the garden; a railway at the bottom of the garden; properties near an electric sub-station, being ex-council; or sited directly on a dual carriageway. Although you may not find a particular feature a put-off, if a significant number of people will, then you are severely limiting your potential buyers on re-sale. If you are not sure if a factor is a turn-off, do a quick survey of your friends.

Make sure that if you are buying somewhere which has a turn-off that it is at least priced appropriately, ie cheaper than if it did not have a turn-off. Bear in mind that if you are buying something cheaper due to a put-off factor, it will sell cheaper as well. The factors that apply to you when you buy something will probably still apply when you sell.

The Expert's Guide to Buying a House in the UK:
helping you to buy a good home and a good property investment.
by Dr Judith Summer.

7.10. Does the survey support your choice?

Any big problems with the structure of the house should be apparent to your surveyor when he does a full survey, which is a big reason why you should not stint on paying for one of these. So don't worry too much about the structure of the building at the first viewing, although be alerted if there are any major and obvious cracks as a surveyor should definitely check these out before a purchase. If the survey reveals big issues, you may want to rethink your purchase or the amount you are prepared to offer.

7.11 Summary top tips

It is a good idea to have an eyes wide open approach to the condition of the property, whether any issue can be dealt with and whether you want to.

The Expert's Guide to Buying a House in the UK:
helping you to buy a good home and a good property investment.
by Dr Judith Summer.

Chapter 8

Other investigations

8.1   The neighbours

8.2   Noise

8.3   Local crime

8.4   Maintenance

8.5   Website searches

8.6   Summary top tips

Once you have decided on a property you want to buy, are there any further investigations you should carry out to know more about what you are letting yourself in for?

8.1   The neighbours

Some people say you should knock on neighbours' doors to get a feel of who you will be living near and ask questions like, "What is it like to live in this area/ road?" I have never done this. People have knocked on my door though and it annoys me. I think, "How dare they judge me!" I know someone who has been put off by meeting their potential neighbours even though they were looking at a detached house. How much information are you really going to glean? How much of an accurate impression are

The Expert's Guide to Buying a House in the UK:
helping you to buy a good home and a good property investment.
by Dr Judith Summer.

---

you going to get? How can you tell by speaking to someone once if her husband is going to annoy you?

So, personally, I would not bother speaking to the neighbours, but you can if you want!

However, that is not to say that you should not gather other hard data about the road and the area, especially if it is not already familiar to you. Other things you might want to know about follow.

8.2. Noise

You should visit the road by day and by night, and at different times of the day and night, to see how it changes. Is it peaceful by day, but a centre for teenagers to meet up by night? Is there a school playground next door making your lunchtimes and other peak times of day noisy, or would that not bother you?

You can usually telephone your local council to find out how to get data on noise complaints in the area over a period of time, say a year. So in this way you can find out if there have been any noise complaints against your potential new neighbours.

http://services.defra.gov.uk/wps/portal/noise has a tool which can help you decide if your chosen location is in a particularly noisy threshold area, for instance if it is close to a motorway.

8.3 Local crime

Crime statistics for any given area are usually also available online eg via http://www.police.uk. You may also want to observe what the lighting in the street is like and whether there is any obvious graffiti.

**The Expert's Guide to Buying a House in the UK:
helping you to buy a good home and a good property investment.
by Dr Judith Summer.**

8.4   Maintenance

Look at the houses nearby. Are they full of graffiti? Are they well maintained? If the house touching yours looks decrepit, you may have problems. Leaks may occur in the property you are looking at due to the bad maintenance of the house next door. And, although of course this is not always the case, you might be more likely to have social problems with the owners of a badly maintained house, or ones who leave old sofas and other rubbish outside their home for long periods of time.

8.5   Website searches

There are a number of online search websites and forums which offer more information about an area or road. I tend not to use these, as I prefer to buy in an area which I have got to know by being physically there and I prefer to look at data as set out above. However, websites and online forums do exist, and if it makes you feel more comfortable, feel free to consult them. I would suggest you do not drive yourself mad with them, nor use them as a substitute to physical visits to the property you wish to buy and its local area.

The most famous website is probably upmystreet.co.uk, but this no longer exists. Here are some others, although I can make no comment as to how useful or reliable they are and how up to date:

http://www.mouseprice.com - You type in the postcode to find out information about a particular property's value compared to others nearby, and there is also an area guide.

http://www.checkmyfile.com - By typing in the postcode to the "Check Any Postcode" tab or to http://www.checkmyarea.com, detailed information comes up about the area's composition, including how credit worthy the area is compared to the rest of the country, its family composition, and the education, employment types, lifestyle and social status of its residents. It even indicates which newspapers the residents tend to read!

**The Expert's Guide to Buying a House in the UK:
helping you to buy a good home and a good property investment.
by Dr Judith Summer.**

---

http://www.neighbourhood.statistics.gov.uk/ - this is another area information site based on postcode and will give information from the last Census, the type of people in the area including things like the make up of the religions and employment status of the people in the area, deprivation, health, local economy, education housing and crime and safety.

http://www.uklocalarea.com/ - this allows a UK postcode search for local area information including census statistics, deprivation index, house prices, school results, public transport, council tax, energy prices and street-level crime in England, Wales and Scotland.

http://www.propertywizza.com/. This is another postcode search based website which provides quite comprehensive local information such as school league tables, Ofsted reports, crime statistics, sold house prices by Zoopla, valuation estimates by MousePrice, council tax, flood risk, pollution reports, neighbourhood statistics, planning applications, local government, local pub guide, local problems and responses, parking, postboxes, affluence, public notices, broadband coverage, doctors and dentists.

https://www.streetcheck.co.uk/ similarly pulls together local information about property and people based on a street or postcode search.

http://www.fixmystreet.com is a website where you can see what problems have been reported to and which have been dealt with by a named council, such as rubbish dumping or loose manholes. You can also report a problem, see all reports for an area or road and set up an alert for when problems are logged.

http://www.ratemyroad.com - allows access to reviews of roads written by local residents. You can also find sold prices, school data and other local information.

http://www.walkscore.com - gives the postcode you type a "walk score", saying how easy it is to do daily errands without a car and what there is in the neighbourhood to walk to, such as restaurants, coffee shops, schools, shops and parks.

**The Expert's Guide to Buying a House in the UK:
helping you to buy a good home and a good property investment.
by Dr Judith Summer.**

---

http://www.maps.google.co.uk. Googlemaps allows you to see some of the things located in the area you are looking at, and its street view function can be useful if you are not so familiar with the area.

http://www.homecheck.co.uk. Based on postcode, this gives information about potential environmental risks, neighbourhood or planning information in the vicinity of the property you are interested in. It also provides information about local crime rates and amenities.

http://www.highways.gov.uk/roads. This is the Highways Agency website and can give you information about planned roads and roadworks. The Scottish version is http://www.transport.gov.scot/road

https://www.planningportal.co.uk/ allows you to search for planning permissions granted in the area either by postcode or council name. It is the UK Government's online planning and building regulations resource for England and Wales,

8.6 Summary top tips

It is good to be aware of the wider picture in the block of flats, road or neighbourhood before you commit, but do not drive yourself mad by looking at every online search system that there is. In any case, nothing beats going to visit the area in person.

The Expert's Guide to Buying a House in the UK:
helping you to buy a good home and a good property investment.
by Dr Judith Summer.

Chapter 9

Bidding for a property

9.1 Factors to consider

9.2 See how the agent responds

9.3 Offers in writing

9.4 How high should you go?

9.5 Final bids

9.6 Mortgage valuation

9.7 Should you be the first bidder?

9.8 Gazumping and moratoriums on marketing/ lock out agreements

9.9 Sealed bids and competitive bids

9.10 Summary top tips

9.1 Factors to consider

Now you know how much the property is worth, you need to make an appropriate bid. There is no easy formula for where you place your first or any bid and there are several factors to take into account, including:

**The Expert's Guide to Buying a House in the UK:
helping you to buy a good home and a good property investment.
by Dr Judith Summer.**

---

1. Is this a frenzied, competitive market, where everyone is fighting tooth and nail for the same property? In which case a low, speculative bid is not going to win.

2. Is the seller motivated to sell eg does he have somewhere to move? In which case he is more likely to wish to negotiate and a speculative bid might be worthwhile.

3. Has the property been on the market a long while? In which case the seller might be getting desperate to sell and might accept a lower bid.

9.2   See how the agent responds

I usually make an offer whilst talking to the agent, and then follow up with a written offer. Whatever you decide your first bid is going to be, listen to see how excited the agent is when you make it. If he starts to talk quicker, you may have got the level right. If it is refused, see if you can get a counter-offer from the seller. If that is the case, he may be aiming to sell at a point midway between your first bid and his counter-offer.

9.3   Offers in writing

Whatever the agent says in response to your verbal offer, always follow up with a detailed written offer. Even if you do not make a verbal offer first, send the agent a detailed written offer. Remember, some deals are won on the particulars of the offer rather than the actual price. If you send your offer by email it is easy for the agent to forward to his client, and that is the surest way you have of reaching the seller with all the information you want to get across. The agent is obliged to put before his client every firm offer received and all its details, although he does not have to just forward your email, whilst in practice he normally would.

So what should you say in your written offer besides the price? Include information such as:

- whether you need a mortgage or you are a cash buyer;

**The Expert's Guide to Buying a House in the UK:
helping you to buy a good home and a good property investment.
by Dr Judith Summer.**

- if you need a mortgage, explain if you already have a mortgage broker appointed and whether you have a mortgage in principle. Obviously having a mortgage broker appointed and a mortgage in principle will make you an attractive purchaser. More on this in other chapters;

- if your purchase is chain free, ie is not dependant upon the sale of another property, tell the seller, as that will also make your bid more attractive.

- if you have solicitors and insurance brokers and anyone else who can help the process lined up, tell the seller.

- tell the seller, if you can, how long you need to exchange and/or complete. This will depend on whether you have a mortgage in principle and solicitors in place.

- tell the seller about yourself. Some sellers really like to know that their property will fall into "good" hands and will be looked after by a nice couple/ family etc. To help get the human connection, introduce yourself in the written offer by telling them about your job and family circumstances. See if you can pull at their heartstrings and make them want to sell to you. (Don't lie though! Only say "I am a teacher, married with a baby on the way and we are looking for our first home together." if that is true!)

- you can also explain the reasons why you have pitched your offer at that level so that the vendor can understand how reasonable you are being. You might, for instance, want to say that similar properties sold in the same road or the same block of flats for a particular price, and list the comparables. It is hard to argue with facts even in the face of an over-enthusiastic estate agent.

A written offer makes you look like a serious buyer and a professional type of person, and it can set you apart from the rest. It makes you memorable both to the estate agent and the vendor and you get to tell the estate agent and the vendor everything you want them to know. Even if your offer is not accepted the first time round, your written offer is the offer that everyone is going to remember if the sale to someone else falls through, and is easily retrievable. So you may find yourself being contacted even if you thought you had lost out on the property.

9.4 How high should you go?

The seller rarely expects your first bid to be your last, so bear this in mind when you make your opening bid.

Do not bid over the level that you can afford. Be prepared to walk away if the bidding goes beyond your budget. I cannot stress this point highly enough. There will be other properties out there eventually which fit your budget and you will have learned from the experience. People get excited by the auction and emotions can run high, but you need to be able to think with your head and not let the auction run away with you.

In one sense, the advertised property price is actually irrelevant, and may be just wishful thinking on the part of the owner. Some estate agents are notorious for over-pricing properties to get business. In a way, the only value that is of true importance is the value that you have put on the property in following the valuation steps above.

Only bid over the level that you have valued the property at if you can afford to, and if there is a good reason why that property is going to be worth more to you; for instance, if you can see a development opportunity, the location is of special importance to you or you are under great pressure to move house. Do not bid over just because someone else has. Their overbid could be their future problem and may make it impossible for them to get a mortgage. Then you will be waiting in the background to step in and an extremely grateful seller may now find your bid acceptable.

9.5 Final bids

It would be helpful if the estate agent knows that your final bid is exactly that. If he can sense that there is more money available from you, he will not be able to advise his client, the seller, to accept your offer. If it really is final, then by all means say so and stick to it. Do not pretend it is your final bid if it isn't as you may lose all credibility with future bidding on this or another property.

The Expert's Guide to Buying a House in the UK:
helping you to buy a good home and a good property investment.
by Dr Judith Summer.

9.6 Mortgage valuation

Bear in mind that the mortgage valuation survey needs to support the agreed purchase price, or at least enough of it for you to be able to get your mortgage. When I say "at least enough of it" I mean that the loan to value ratio has to be met.

So say you have a property price agreed at £100,000, you have £40,000 and you need to borrow £60,000. If your mortgage company's loan to value rate is 75%, then it will lend you 75% of the mortgage valuation, not 75% of the agreed purchase price. So even if the mortgage valuation comes in at say £90,000. which is lower than the purchase price agreed, you will still be able to borrow your £60,000. Because 75% of 90,000 is £67,500. You can still borrow the £60,000 you want as it is less than £67,500.

9.7 Should you be the first bidder?

This is a tricky question and the answer will depend on the circumstances. The problem with being the first bidder is that there is a risk that an agent could tell another bidder what figure they would need to beat to win the deal. Often an estate agent will be happy to tell you whether there are other bids, but not what they are, and before you bid you should ask if there are already other bids on the table. This should inform your level of bid, ie whether you should bid speculatively or at the true valuation bracket that you have worked out. Sometimes an agent will hint at what numbers to beat, or what the seller would find acceptable. Of course the number you are told is acceptable may not be the <u>lowest</u> acceptable number! The agent will usually tell you the amount of a bid which has been rejected already.

I think that if you refrain from bidding just because you do not want to be the first bidder, there is a good chance that you will miss out and that someone else's bid will be accepted before you get a chance to compete. There are times where the first bidder will win the bid, especially if the seller does not want to put the property on the open market. Sometimes a seller prefers a first bidder, even if a second bidder comes in with the same offer. If there is no-one else on the horizon making a bid, then you will have an advantage in making a first bid. The seller may still want to wait and see

The Expert's Guide to Buying a House in the UK:
helping you to buy a good home and a good property investment.
by Dr Judith Summer.

---

if any other offer comes in, but the more bleak the horizon, the more likely you are to succeed in even a speculative bid.

There is less of a disadvantage in putting in the first bid if you have done valuation research and your bid is within a sensible true valuation range. The estate agent advising the seller will advise them whether yours is a fair bid or not, and it is your fair bid that everyone else is going to have to compete with, and that will be a difficult competition.

If you decide not to be the first bidder, make sure you tell the agent that you intend to bid, so that he may give you a chance to compete.

9.8 Gazumping and moratoriums on marketing/ lock out agreements

If you make an offer on the property which is accepted, you can and should ask the seller to take the property off the market. They do not have to. If they refuse, are you still buying it? Probably. You are at risk that a new buyer will come along and bid higher ie that you will be gazumped. However, the risk is less if yours is a true market value bid and you do everything you can do to progress the purchase.

Even if the seller does take a property off the market, or agree not to show it to any new applicant, they won't do so for long. They may give you a period of say two weeks - a moratorium - where they agree not to show the property to anyone new, although, of course, someone who has seen the property before might come along with an offer. And who is to prove whether they actually saw the property before or after the so-called moratorium?

Sometimes lock out agreements are proposed which formalise the position. My experience is that they are hardly worth the paper they are written on, as a seller who does not wish to sell to you can just wait until the moratorium period agreed has passed before selling to someone else if he is convinced there is another serious buyer out there with more money. I have also found that a huge amount of time, effort and solicitors' costs can be incurred in banging out the details, when during that time the property is still being marketed, and could have been exchanged!

**The Expert's Guide to Buying a House in the UK:
helping you to buy a good home and a good property investment.
by Dr Judith Summer.**

Whether or not there is a lock out agreement or some sort of moratorium, you can still get gazumped even if a property is no longer being advertised or viewed - by someone making a higher offer than you. That person may have seen the property advertised and may have viewed it earlier. Every agent has an obligation to pass on to the seller every offer made on the property.

The seller will need to see you spending money eg on mortgage valuation fees and surveyors before they are happy to keep it off the market for a longer period of time and also to be persuaded to stick with you as the buyer even if they receive a higher offer.

If a higher offer comes in and you are gazumped, you can still fight back and at least match the other offer, but only if you believe the property to be worth more and if you can afford to spend more. Do not get carried away. If you are able to match the other offer, it may be that the sellers will decide to stick with you, rather than the new offeror. You might not need to beat the new offer, but just match it. Remember the speed at which you can get the contracts finalised and exchanged will probably be an important factor to the seller, and you may have the advantage over the other buyer if you have already started the purchasing process ahead of him.

You have more chance of getting gazumped if multiple agents are involved. This is because the agents want to earn fees for their agencies and personal commission for themselves. If there are multiple agents, the fee that the seller pays is split with the other agents. Usually the agent with the successful buyer gets a greater percentage of the fee than the other agents. Sometimes the other agent or agents will get nothing. So with a multiple agency, an agent might be more interested in finding a buyer to gazump the winning bid and give him a chance, if the new bid is accepted, of his earning a fee or a bigger fee.

It is not really in the estate agent's interest to get you gazumped if he is the only agent. This is because he wants a fee as quickly as possible and he will get a fee if he sells the property. It is true that if a gazumping occurs and a higher amount is accepted, he will earn a slightly higher fee, but usually the difference for him in selling the property at a slightly higher price following a gazumping is only worth a very little extra fee. It is not worth him risking losing the sale altogether through the first buyer

The Expert's Guide to Buying a House in the UK:
helping you to buy a good home and a good property investment.
by Dr Judith Summer.

being gazumped and finding something else to buy, and then the second buyer's purchase falling through.

So in summary, you are safer from getting gazumped if there is only one agent. But to keep the seller interested in you, he has to see that you are serious in progressing quickly, and that you are committed enough to spend money eg on the valuation fees/surveyor. You might even want to pay down a token advance payment or deposit.

On the flip side, if you want to make a bid on a property which is already under offer, go ahead: what do you have to lose? At best your offer may be accepted, although you may have a contract race on your hands - a situation where two parties compete to get to exchange of contracts first. At worst, your offer is refused but you are next in line should the first buyer be unable to go through with the purchase, for instance if his mortgage falls through.

9.9 Sealed bids and competitive bids

Sometimes there are two or more bidders fighting for the same property and the seller (advised by his estate agent) suggests sealed bids. This means that each bidder will have to write down his offer by a certain time, and the seller will decide between them. If you are in this situation, you need to put forward your best bid, based on your valuation of the property.

You will need to add information about yourself to explain why your bid should be accepted and why you are a better bidder than anyone else. There are factors which make a difference to a seller other than the price, including your personal position and how you intend to fund the purchase. So you must say if you are chain free, if you are a cash buyer or if you have a mortgage in principle etc. Also say how long you need to exchange and complete. Some sellers also want to know if you intend to use the property for yourself or if you are a developer, and will prefer not to sell to a developer, even if the developer offers more money. Some sellers are swayed by the personal side of your story if there is one. For instance, with two equal bids, I have seen an example where the seller chose the buyer with the disabled child who needed ground floor direct access to the roadside.

The Expert's Guide to Buying a House in the UK:
helping you to buy a good home and a good property investment.
by Dr Judith Summer.

In any situation where you are competing in a bid, the more information they have about you that shows you to be an attractive bidder, the better your chances.

If I have been in a competitive bid before now, I have added up to £5,000 to the number I was going to bid to sweeten it and make me more likely to succeed. People like to work to the nearest 25 thousand. So if I think that the competitor's bid is going to be £750,000, I might bid £755,000 if I can afford it. Similarly if I think the competitor's bid is going to be £500,000, I might bid £505,000. Just a little trick that I think has won me a number of contracts over the years.

If you do not win in a competitive situation, be prepared to walk away. The world has not ended and no-one died!

9.10 Summary top tips

Once you have decided the value of the property, make a sensible bid, but decide in advance what your limit is and stick to it. Don't get carried away! Put your detailed offer in writing and if it is accepted, move the buying process along as quickly as possible.

The Expert's Guide to Buying a House in the UK:
helping you to buy a good home and a good property investment.
by Dr Judith Summer.

Chapter 10

How to buy a house if you are in a chain

10.1 What is a chain?

10.2 Advantages of being chain free

10.3 Disadvantages of making yourself chain free

10.4 How to keep your end of the chain in motion

10.5 Bridging finance

10.6 Summary top tips

10.1 What is a chain?

More often than not, if you are not a first time buyer, you will have a property to sell before you will able to buy so you can use the proceeds of the sale of the first home to buy the next one. If you want your sale to go through at the same time as your purchase, you will be in a chain. And the person buying your house may be dependant on the sale of his own house, and so the chain goes on. The whole chain of sales and purchases can be broken by just one person not being able to complete a sale.

10.2 Advantages of being chain free

If you are chain free, there are advantages:

The Expert's Guide to Buying a House in the UK:
helping you to buy a good home and a good property investment.
by Dr Judith Summer.

---

1. You should be able to move forward on buying a new home quickly;

2. You should be more able to compete against cash buyers;

3. You won't miss out because of the chain breaking down on the sale of your property;

4. You will have certainty in knowing the amount you have to spend

5. All this makes your buying offer attractive - maybe even if you offer a purchase price at an amount less than a chained person.

10.3 Disadvantages of making yourself chain free

But in spite of all this, I would not choose to sell first and make myself chain free before buying. Firstly, there are disadvantages in doing this, and secondly, if handled right you should be able to sell and purchase in a chain like the rest of the 67% of purchasers.

The disadvantages of selling your home before you have found somewhere to buy include:

1. You have to live somewhere. Do you really want to move back to your parents? Or are you going to rent? Rentals under 3 months are hard to find and there is an additional expenditure here.

2. Moving house twice in a short space of time can be disruptive, especially if children are involved. Please do not underestimate the effect that moving has on children of all ages.

3. What if you do not find somewhere, and then get priced out of the market?

The Expert's Guide to Buying a House in the UK:
helping you to buy a good home and a good property investment.
by Dr Judith Summer.

10.4 How to try to keep your end of the chain in motion

What I would advise to try to keep your end of the chain in motion:

1. Put your home up for sale and see what the interest is like and at what price levels.

2. Hold off agreeing a sale until you find something else or agree a long completion date for your sale eg 6 months - if all else fails you can rent at the end of the long completion date.

3. Up the effort in finding a new house.

4. If you find somewhere you wish to buy, be prepared to accept a lower offer on your house to be able to get the timing right.

Bear in mind:

1. If you lose out on a purchase, it is not actually the end of the world. There will be another house out there.

2. When a seller is sizing up potential bids, a chained purchaser who has a buyer can be just as attractive a prospect as a cash buyer if the money being offered is right.

10.5 Bridging finance

There may be financing available to you if you have a gap between your purchase and your sale so that you will have to buy the property before completing on your sale. This is called bridging finance and is usually very expensive and is only available on a relatively short term basis. It is risky. For all these reasons it should not be considered unless you really have to, and even then only for a very short period. Specialist companies offer bridging finance, but you will probably be much safer to go through a mortgage broker.

The Expert's Guide to Buying a House in the UK:
helping you to buy a good home and a good property investment.
by Dr Judith Summer.

10.6 Summary top tips

Being in a chain can make the process of buying harder for you, but it is not the end of the world, and does not mean that you cannot succeed in selling the property you are living in at the same time as buying a new one.

The Expert's Guide to Buying a House in the UK:
helping you to buy a good home and a good property investment.
by Dr Judith Summer.

Chapter 11

Development

11.1 Buying with a development in mind

11.2 Permissions

11.3 Enhancing the value

11.4 Neutral decor

11.5 Development for own use or for re-sale

11.6 Summary top tips

11.1 Buying with a development in mind

Do not buy somewhere speculatively if you <u>only</u> want it if you can do a certain development. So for instance, do not buy a house which needs a loft extension else it will be too small for your family, unless you know you will be able to build a loft extension. You will need to have lined up a Plan B which is acceptable to you as well. Plan B might be to own the property without doing the development, or to be able to do a lesser development for which you know for sure that you have or will have permission. Hoping you will get permission is not the same as knowing for sure. You have either to be happy with Plan B, or find out definitively before you commit whether you will be able to do what you would like to the property under your Plan A. In the case of a flat, you should be able to find out from the management company or other freeholders in advance what the regulations in the building allow, although they

The Expert's Guide to Buying a House in the UK:
helping you to buy a good home and a good property investment.
by Dr Judith Summer.

---

may not provide the information quickly enough, which might mean you lose out on the purchase. And the flat's regulations may change without warning.

11.2 Permissions

Bear in mind that you will need planning permission for much of what you might want to do to a property, and freeholders' permission in addition for a flat. Properties in a conservation area will have extra restrictions and listed properties will have even more. If the property is leasehold, there may be some terms (covenants) in the lease forbidding certain developments or requiring that you first seek permission from another party.

You may be able to obtain general information about permissions of the type you would like from the local council before you purchase, but you may not be able to rely on this information.

Do not presume that you will be able to cut down any tree you want to: some trees are protected by Tree Preservation Orders, and some by being within a conservation area. Any cutting or pruning of them will require permission.

Do not carry out works without getting the appropriate permissions: that is a risky business. At worst you will be required to put the property back as it was before. At best you will have a problem on re-sale.

Certain works can be done without requiring planning permission because they are "permitted development." But do not presume that what you propose falls within the permitted development category. You can check the rules for what counts as permitted development in your area with an online search. These rules change from time and time and can be complicated if other work has already been done to the property over the years. You can also apply to the council to ask for confirmation that the changes you propose will indeed be within the permitted development regulations. As far as I am aware, a flat cannot have permitted development; only a house can after it has been made into a house.

The Expert's Guide to Buying a House in the UK:
helping you to buy a good home and a good property investment.
by Dr Judith Summer.

All structural work requires building control certification to show that it was carried out appropriately. You are meant to contact building control before structural work commences (either via your local council's planning department or you can appoint a private company). Even assuming the structural integrity of the property is sound and the work has been done to the appropriate standard, at the least, you will have a problem on re-sale if you do not obtain the appropriate building control certificate. If building control find out about works, even works which have not been notified to them, they can insist on an inspection, even if it means digging up a tiled floor to look at whether the foundations underneath were built adequately.

You can usually search online via the appropriate council website or https://www.planningportal.co.uk to see the more recent planning applications and permissions which have been granted, rejected or withdrawn in relation to the property you are trying to buy or those surrounding it. This will be important if an application has been withdrawn or rejected and it is the kind of thing which you would also want to do to the property you are buying, for instance an extension. Although some or all of the planning history of the property may come to light via your solicitor's searches, if doing certain work to the property you have in mind is essential for you to want to buy it, then you should look at the planning position before you incur solicitors' fees.

You will also want to check that any work already done to the property was done with planning permission and was certified by building control as necessary. You may wish to check the estate agent's plan against any lease plan or planning permission information you have. Some of this information may become apparent to your solicitor, but you can always ask your solicitor to raise a specific enquiry of the seller if you know particular works have been done to the property, for instance asking whether a specific extension was carried out with planning permission or whether building control ever certified the removal of an internal wall. If you are buying a house which has had structural work done to it, such as moving a supporting wall to make the kitchen/living room open plan, or adding an extension, your solicitor should be asking to see the building control final certificate and telling you about it. Do not contact the local authority directly to ask about any work which may have been done without planning permission, as this would invalidate any future indemnity policy that your solicitor may arrange to protect you from the costs of the local authority taking

any enforcement action to put the property back into the state it was in before unauthorised work was done.

11.3 Enhancing the value

There are things that you can do which will enhance the value of a property. The biggest difference you could make would be to add square footage for instance with a loft conversion, back and/or side house extension and building a conservatory. Basements are expensive to install, but in the most expensive areas they will make a huge difference to the value of the property. Converting the garage into a room may also enhance the value, unless parking in the area is difficult. Especially if parking in the area is in short supply, it may be worth paving over a driveway so as to provide parking.

A new kitchen and new bathrooms can give a major boost to the value of the property. Fitting smart new double-glazing to replace old single panes is an instant winner, but the replacements should reflect the age and style of the property. Installing a glass sliding, folding door along the whole of a back wall into a garden is a popular move, along with night lights for the garden. Sprucing up the front of a house is always a good idea too.

Other value enhancing work might include re-distributing the space to make better use of it, finding a way to use an unused space or adding an appropriate number of WC's/ bathrooms/ shower rooms. Make sure there is at least one bath in a house - at least one bathroom should have a bath, even if you only ever take showers. If you want to remove bedrooms, will the property have enough bedrooms to be easy to re-sell? Will the rooms be too small if you split them up so as to make more rooms? Ask the estate agents through whom you are buying the property for their opinions on the value if you carry out certain works. Get the opinions of more than one agent.

Bear in mind that the professional property developer will have already made his profit by buying at a discount, and/or he will know the value against the cost of the improvements he will want to make. He will not be relying on house prices rising, and nor should you.

The Expert's Guide to Buying a House in the UK:
helping you to buy a good home and a good property investment.
by Dr Judith Summer.

11.4 Neutral decor

Whatever you decide to do, if you are likely to resell in the not too distant future, keep the decor neutral, and put splashes of colour in by way of accessories or paint accents. The effect on the room is usually enough, but it is cheaper to change accessories or paint one wall than it is for instance, to re-tile an inappropriately coloured bathroom.

11.5 Development for own use or for re-sale

If you want to develop a house primarily for your own use and enjoyment, for instance by building a loft extension so you can have the extra bedroom you need, then the value it might add to the property is a secondary issue, although try not to spend more than the value you will be adding to your house. Similarly if you are going to be in the property for many years to come, you do not need to be so careful about choosing neutral decor.

If you are going to buy and develop something for re-sale, you need to know what you are doing and exactly which market you are aiming for and stick tightly to a budget. Make sure the cost of the development can be recouped with profit at the time of the re-sale. Despite popular television programmes making property development seem like something anyone can do, like anything else in life, a successful property developer needs a certain amount of skill, sense and know how. There will also be tax issues to consider when thinking of selling a development property.

11.6 Summary top tips

Not everyone is Sarah Beeny, although I suspect lots of people think they can be. Not all property development ends with a shiny house and a fat profit. Property prices can fall, and developers cannot rely on a market rise for a profit - the profit should come from the added value that the development gives to the property. Take care with making purchases which only make sense for you if you are allowed to carry out a certain development. Make sure all necessary permissions are in place before you start any building work, and make sure you get the appropriate building control certificates afterwards. If work has already been done before you purchase the

**The Expert's Guide to Buying a House in the UK:
helping you to buy a good home and a good property investment.
by Dr Judith Summer.**

---

property, make sure the appropriate permissions and building control certificates were granted. If not, speak to your solicitor about obtaining an indemnity. Try not to spend more on a development than the value that it adds to your property. Keep decor neutral unless you are going to live in the property for a long while.

Maybe I should write another book on property development!

Chapter 12

The conveyancing process

12.1 How long do you need to find a property?

12.2 Exchange and completion in England and Wales

12.3 Things that slow down exchange

12.4 Two week exchanges

12.5 Contract race

12.6 Summary top tips

12.1 How long do you need to find a property?

When you start your search, you may be lucky and find something suitable which is already on the market, just waiting for you to come along. That would be nice. But it may take you 6 months or even a year in areas where there is limited housing stock. You have to stay focused on your search and realistic in your expectations. If it is taking you a very long time, ask yourself if you or your partner really want to move at all. Be patient. But you have to be active in your search.

Bear in mind that more properties come to the market in spring and September, and that it may be easier to pick up a bargain for properties which have been hanging around a while if they are still on the market in August or December.

The Expert's Guide to Buying a House in the UK:
helping you to buy a good home and a good property investment.
by Dr Judith Summer.

12.2 Exchange and completion in England and Wales

How long should the process of buying take once an offer has been accepted? In short, it can take on average 6-10 weeks before you get the keys, but it can easily be quicker or slower depending on the circumstances. In England and Wales, there is a two part process to the conveyancing: 1. exchange (this could take 4-6 weeks on average) and 2. completion (which should not take more than 2/3 weeks after that).

Exchange is the moment when you commit to buying the property at the date set out as the completion date. Completion is when you finally own the property and can have the keys. Before exchange, both you (ie your solicitor) and your mortgage provider have to carry out investigations and once everyone is satisfied that all is in order, then you can exchange contracts and commit to the purchase. The actual process of exchange and completion is carried out by your solicitor. You may be asked to sign the relevant documents, arrange a surveyor, provide the money at the right time and answer your solicitors' queries.

12.3 Things that slow down exchange

1. *Mortgages.* The process will be much quicker if you do not need a mortgage, but if you do you can speed up the process by having your mortgage provider lined up and if you have a mortgage in principle, which basically means that you are approved for a loan of a certain amount. This means that the mortgage provider will only have to send round a property valuer to confirm that the property has enough value to secure the loan before it makes a formal offer. You need to be on top of the mortgage provider (via the mortgage broker if you have one) to make sure they do this and that the valuer gets the information back to the mortgage provider quickly.

Unless and until you are sure that you will get the mortgage you want on the property you are bidding for, I would suggest that you ask your solicitor to incur minimum costs. This would mean delaying his review of the sale papers and even delaying requesting the local searches (see below) until you have a mortgage offer, or at least until you have an indication that you are likely to get an mortgage offer. For there is no point paying for your solicitor's fees on doing the work necessary for the purchase of the property, if you are not going to get the mortgage you need to buy that

**The Expert's Guide to Buying a House in the UK:
helping you to buy a good home and a good property investment.
by Dr Judith Summer.**

---

property. If you go down this route, be sure to make it very clear to the estate agent from the beginning what you are doing, so no-one is misled about the timing and the seller does not think you are delaying because you are going to pull out of the purchase. If your local authority is known to take a long time to provide the searches, then you may have to incur the costs of ordering these at an early stage, even if you ask your solicitor not to review them until the mortgage offer has come through. If the deal is under time pressure, you may not have the luxury of waiting for your mortgage offer before asking your solicitor to proceed, but you take a risk. It would be better to be open and negotiate the time you actually need.

2. *Finding a solicitor.* Looking for a suitable solicitor could take time. But that is something that is easy to line up before you even view your first property. Ask for recommendations from friends and family or the estate agent may suggest someone. Solicitors should be able to give you quotations in advance for helping you with a purchase of a specified sort of size. Solicitors from smaller firms usually cost less than those from bigger firms, and in urban areas such as London there is a big difference in cost between high street, West End and City firms, although sometimes you can tell a big difference in the service too.

3. *Local searches.* Some councils respond to requests from your solicitor for searches in 48 hours; others take 6-8 weeks. Sometimes you can attend in person or your solicitor can which costs more but would speed up the process.

4. *Insurance.* House insurance needs to be lined up too, and some mortgage providers require it to be in place before they will lend any money. So it is a good idea to start getting quotations as soon as an offer is accepted. Too often this becomes a last minute rush around.

5. *Money transfers.* Money transfers can also delay the process. You will usually have to provide 10% of the purchase price on exchange and the rest on completion. The mortgage provider only usually lends on completion, so if you do not have 10% available at the time of exchange, you will need to negotiate that less is payable on exchange. Make sure you transfer your monies in time. You may have to transfer them into a current account first, and then get them to the solicitor. Speak to your bank about their processes and timing. Sometimes a transfer can take 5 working days. Also get your solicitor to check when the mortgage provider will be sending the

money. I recently had an experience where the mortgage provider did not want to release the monies until 3pm, which is far too late considering that usually you contract to get the money to the seller by 2pm!

6. *Chain.* If you are reliant on a chain, then it is important to wait until everyone in the chain is ready for a simultaneous exchange and later completion. If one person is delayed on your chain, then you will also be delayed. There are interest penalties if you are unable to complete at the time you commit to complete, even if the delay is not your fault, but the fault of someone else on your chain.

12.4 Two week exchanges

Sometimes, especially in London, or in other areas where there is huge competition, a 2 week exchange is not uncommon. This is not impossible if you have your ducks lined up, and if the seller provides a complete set of information in the first place, but it may be hard to get your mortgage provider to work quickly enough. If this deadline is within reach, then go for it, but keep the estate agent updated as to progress, especially if there are any delays.

It is in everyone's interest for the sale to go through, and if the seller believes you are serious, he might well extend any deadline, especially if you agree to shorten the completion time to compensate. It is even possible to exchange and complete in one day, although I do not recommend a rush unless there is really good reason. The key is to keep the estate agent informed of progress so that everyone's expectations are managed.

12.5 Contract race

If there are two bids at the same price and the seller cannot decide between them, he may just say that the first one who can get to exchange will win the property. Contract races are nasty as both the winner and the loser will have to incur expenses, for instance their solicitors' fees. I am not sure I would be happy to take part in one, and I have always discouraged any suggestion of one.

The Expert's Guide to Buying a House in the UK:
helping you to buy a good home and a good property investment.
by Dr Judith Summer.

12.6 Summary top tips

The purchase process can take a couple of months and is different in Scotland. Line up your "team" and any mortgage in principle in advance and do not stall else you may lose the purchase. Keep the estate agent informed of progress and delays so that he can pass on the information to the seller and keep the seller convinced you are committed to the process. Avoid accepting unrealistic deadlines or making macho deadline statements.

The Expert's Guide to Buying a House in the UK:
helping you to buy a good home and a good property investment.
by Dr Judith Summer.

Epilogue

I thought I would conclude with a couple of my mantras:

1. You do not have to get the best deal in the universe, just the deal that is good for you and works for you.

2. Property is just bricks and mortar - if you lose out on a sale or purchase, it is not the end of the world and no-one has died. Keep things in perspective.

Good luck on your property journey! :)

Please contact me if you think I can help you further via:

http://www.simmaproperties.co.uk

www.ingramcontent.com/pod-product-compliance
Lightning Source LLC
Chambersburg PA
CBHW070109210526
45170CB00013B/802